Academy of Business Research

Program for the Academy of Business Research

Spring 2011

March 16-18, 2011

Iberville Suites

New Orleans, LA

Conference Program[*]

[*]The conference proceedings will be published and indexed by April 1st on the Social Science Resource Network (SSRN)

Sponsors and Supporters

Academy of Business Research would like to thank
the following companies and organizations
for sponsoring the Spring 2011 Conference:

AACSB International

Amazon.com

American Finance Association

Cabells Publishing (www.cabells.com)

Coldwell Banker

Decision Sciences Institute

European Financial Management Association

Financial Management Association

Journal of Finance

Sentina Publishing

Silver Wheaton

Social Science Resource Network

Trump Entertainment International

Conference Staff

Conference Chair

Randall Valentine, Ph.D.

Support Staff

Neelam Kumar Dhungel

Candace Driggers

Harrison Enfinger

Zach Hayes

Archie Seymer

Ashley Seymer

Conference Social Activities

Registration: 8:30-3:00 Daily

Uptown Room

Wednesday 5:00-6:30 PM

Reception with Cash Bar

Carrolton Room

Thursday 7:00-8:00 AM

Doctoral Student Breakfast

Grand Lobby at Iberville Suites

Thursday 6:00 PM

Awards Dinner at Oceana Grill

(on corner of Bourbon and Conti)

*Complimentary Continental Breakfast for all Hotel Guests

Journal Special Editions

Academy of Business Journal

The *Academy of Business Journal* will publish a special edition for papers focusing on the global financial crisis in Fall 2011. **Article submissions are due by May 1.**

The *Academy of Business Journal* will publish a special edition for papers focusing on issues in strategic management in Spring 2012. **Article submissions are due September 1.**

Journal of Applied Financial Research

The *Journal of Applied Financial Research* will publish a special edition for papers focusing on international banking and finance in Fall 2011. **Article submissions are due July 1.**

Future Conference Dates

Academy of Business Research

Fall 2011 Meeting

Trump Plaza Atlantic City, NJ

September 13-15

Academy of Business Research

Winter 2011 Meeting

Planet Hollywood Las Vegas, NV

November 14-16

www.academyofbusinessresearch.com

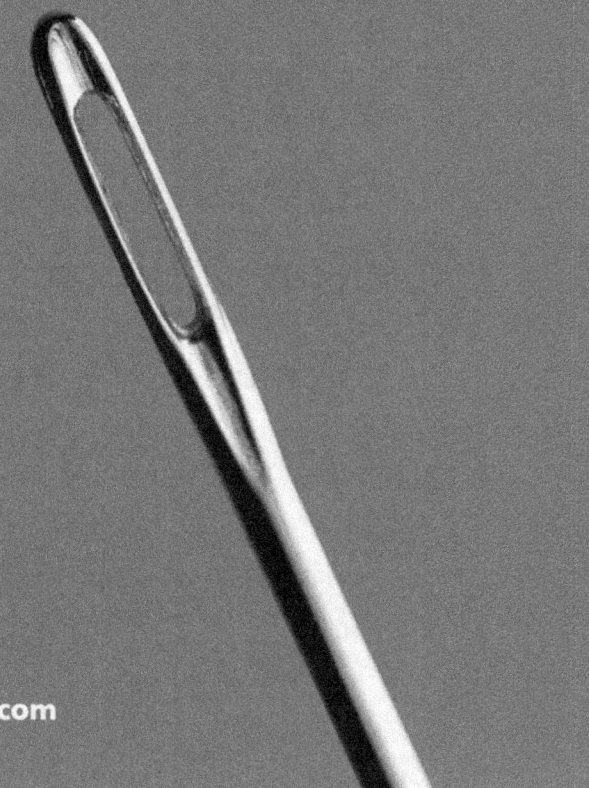

9:30 AM Wednesday March 16th

Carrollton Room

Sponsor: Silver Wheaton

Economics

Session Chair: John Levandis, Loyola University New Orleans

RELIGIOUS FRACTIONALIZATION AND ECONOMIC GROWTH: A BAYESIAN ERRORS-IN-VARIABLES MODEL

John Levandis, Loyola University New Orleans

THE IMPACT OF MISSOURI'S MINIMUM WAGE INCREASE ON LOW WAGE WORKERS

Diane Primont, Southeast Missouri State University
Rebecca Summary, Southeast Missouri State University

IMPACT OF BALANCE OF PAYMENT AND INTEREST RATES ON INFLATION IN PAKISTAN

Hammad Amjad, Central Punjab University Pakistan
Bilal Ilyas, Central Punjab University Pakistan
Zubair Safdar, Central Punjab University Pakistan
Ali Pervaiz, Central Punjab University Pakistan

PERFORMANCE OR PROFIT: MAJOR LEAGUE BASEBALL TEAM FINANCIAL MANAGERS FACE TOUGH CHOICES

Susan Logan Nelson, University of North Dakota

Session Chair: Reza Samizadeh, Al'Zahra University, Iran

LEVERAGING A STANDARD DOCUMENTATION FOR ENHANCING THE EFFICIENCY AND EFFECTIVENESS OF SOFTWARE TESTING

Saeed Jahanyan, Tarbiat Modares University, Iran
Reza Samizadeh, Al'Zahra University, Iran

THE MODERATING EFFECT OF TECHNOLOGY ON STUDENT AND INSTRUCTOR VARIABLES ON STUDENT SATISFACTION IN E-LEARNING

Joe Teng, Troy University

A CASE STUDY: ENHANCEMENT OF BUSINESS PROCESS MANAGEMENT THROUGH SYSTEM AUTOMATION

Rachid Belmasrour, Southern University at New Orleans
Muhammed Miah, Southern University at New Orleans
Adnan Omar, Southern University at New Orleans

DISCRETE TIME MODEL FOR AGGREGATE MORTGAGE DEFAULT RISK

Feng Xu, Georgia Southwestern State University
Refik Soyer, George Washington University

Carrollton Room

Sponsor: Academy of Business Journal

Finance—Global Financial Crisis

Session Chair: Randall Valentine, Academy of Business Research

PROXY FOR CREDIBILITY OF INFLATION POLICY AND UNCERTAINTY OF INFLATION: PANEL EVIDENCE FROM EMERGING ECONOMIES

Hermann Sintim-Aboagye, Montclair State University
Serapio Byekwaso, Verispan University
Chandana Chakraborty, Montclair State University

RISK-TAKING, FINANCIAL DISTRESS AND INNOVATION

Arnav Sheth, St. Mary's College of California
Larry Shepp, Rutgers University
Oded Palmon, Rutgers University

THE TRANSMISSION OF MONETARY POLICY TO NON-BANKING SOURCES OF CREDIT: A LOOK AT COMMERCIAL PAPER MARKET ACTIVITY

Karl D. Boulware, University of Alabama
Robert R. Reed, University of Alabama

THE IMPACT OF TECHNOLOGICAL IMPROVEMENTS ON DEVELOPING FINANCIAL MARKETS: THE CASE OF THE JOHANNESBURG STOCK EXCHANGE

Mehmet F. Dicle, Loyola University of New Orleans
John Levendis, Loyola University of New Orleans

12:30 PM Wednesday March 16th

Esplanade Room

Sponsor: Cabells

Accounting and Marketing

Session Chair: Lawrence R. Hudack, Troy University

THE CASE OF THE MISSING EMPLOYEES: THE SAGA OF FEDEX

Tina Quinn, Arkansas State University
Sam Pae, Arkansas State University

USING THE DUPONT FINANCIAL RATIO ANALYSIS TO EVALUATE THE EFFECT FROM FUNDING CUTS ON SOUTHEASTERN PUBLIC UNIVERSITIES

Lawrence R. Hudack, Troy University
Beverly J. Strachan, Troy University
James A. Deloach, Troy University

THE EFFECTIVENESS OF OUTDOOR LED ADVERTISING SIGNS

Hennie van Bulck, University of South Carolina Sumter

CULTURAL FRAGMENTATION AND GLOBAL SEGMENTATION: THE TWAIN SHALL MEET

Russell Adams, University of Texas Brownsville

2:40 PM Wednesday March 16th

Esplanade Room

Sponsor: Silver Wheaton

Business Education

Session Chair: Dawn Valentine, Georgia Southwestern State University

SUBSTITUTES OR COMPLEMENTS: TEACHING AND SCHOLARSHIP FOR THE ACTIVE SCHOLAR

Blakely Fox Fender, Millsaps College
Susan Washburn Taylor, Millsaps College
Kimberly Gladden Burke, Millsaps College

VALUE MITOSIS – A METHODOLOGY TO DEVELOP COMMUNITY EMPOWERMENT

Michael D. Whitt, Miami Dade College
Nathalie A L Duval-Couetil, Miami Dade College
Rodney G. Handy, Miami Dade College
Satish C. Boregowda, Miami Dade College
Patrick Senarith, Miami Dade College

WOMEN LEADERS

Patsy Parker, Southwestern Oklahoma State University

SOCIAL NETWORKING: THE NEW INNOVATION FOR TARGETING UNDECIDEDS FOR BUSINESS SPECIFIC DISCIPLINES

Rickey Warner, Grambling State University

8:00 AM Thursday March 17th

Gentilly Room

Sponsor: Cabells Publishing

Management

Session Chair: Randall Valentine, Academy of Business Research

THE MODERATING EFFECT OF U.S. REGIONAL COLLECTIVISM ON ACQUIRED FAMILY FIRM SUCCESS

Robert W. Reich, Kennesaw State University

STRATEGIES TO PROMOTE SUSTAINABLE DEVELOPMENT OF INDUSTRIAL PARKS IN VIETNAM'S NORTHERN KEY ECONOMIC ZONE

Huong T. Vu, National Economics University
Long Pham, New Mexico State University

NEGOTIAUCTION

Long Pham, New Mexico State University
Thang Tran, National Economics University

EX-OFFENDERS, FAMILY OWNED FIRMS, AND ENTREPRENEURS: A STUDY OF SIGNALS

Keith E. Ferguson, Kennesaw State University
David L. Williams, Kennesaw State University

8:00 AM Thursday March 17th

Esplanade Room

Sponsor: Trump Plaza

Marketing

Session Chair: H. Richard Priesmeyer, St. Mary's University

THE EMOTIONAL VALUE OF PRODUCTS AND SERVICES: COMPUTING THE VALUE OF EMOTIONAL UTILITY

H. Richard Priesmeyer, St. Mary's University

PRICE TRANSPARENCY AND INFORMATION STRATEGY IN THE AIRLINE INDUSTRY

Terrance J. Kearney, Chicago State University
Richard Robinson, Marquette University

PRIOR RELATIONSHIPS, THE PSYCHOLOGICAL CONTRACT, & SERVICE FAILURE: IT ISN'T ALL ROSES

Venessa Funches, Auburn University Montgomery

THE IMPACT OF PERCEPTION FACTORS ON CONSUMER REACTION UNDER PRODUCT RECALLS

Hee-Kwon Jung, Black Hills State University

THE EFFECTS OF MULTIPLE SOURCES AND PRICE VARIATIONS ON CREATING CONFUSION IN THE CONSUMER DECISION MAKING PROCESS

Komal Gyani Karani, Lamar University
Katherine A. Fraccastoro, Lamar University

INTELLIGENCE IN THE PERSONAL SELLING FIELD

Doug Russell, Northwest Missouri State University
Jim Walker, Northwest Missouri State University

10:00 AM Thursday March 17th

Carrollton Room

Sponsor: Planet Hollywood Las Vegas

International Management

Session Chair: Seyed-Mohammad Seyed Hosseini, IUST

WHEN PROFESSIONAL SERVICE FIRMS INTERNATIONALIZE – CREATING THE BIG PICTURE

Soren Henning Jensen, Copenhagen Business School
Flemming Poulfelt, Copenhagen Business School

DIRECT AND INDIRECT EFFECT OF WORK FAMILY CONFLICT AND FAMILY WORK CONFLICT ON JOB STRESS AND JOB PERFORMANCE

Ayesha Saleem, University of Central Punjab

FACTORS THAT INFLUENCE EXPATRIATE COMPENSATION PROBLEMS

Semere Haile, Grambling State University
Donna Williams, Grambling State University

A NEW BI-OBJECTIVE MATHEMATICAL MODEL FOR OPTIMIZATION OF SUPPLY CHAIN PLANNING ISSUES

Seyed-Mohammad Seyed Hosseini, Iran University of Science and Technology
Behin Elahi, Iran University of Science and Technology
Ahmad Makui, Iran University of Science and Technology

PROPOSING A MATHEMATICAL PROGRAMMING MODEL FOR OPTIMIZATION OF SUPPLY CHAIN SCHEDULING

Seyed-Mohammad Seyed Hosseini, Iran University of Science and Technology
Behin Elahi, Iran University of Science and Technology
Ahmad Makui, Iran University of Science and Technology

THE IMPACT OF URBANIZATION ON FERTILITY AMONG THE IGBOS OF NIGERIA, WEST AFRICA

Remigius U. Onwumere, St. Louis University
James F. Gilsinan, St. Louis University
Emmanuel Uwalaka, St. Louis University

10:00 AM Thursday March 17th
Gentilly Room

Sponsor: Sentina Publishing

Business Education

Session Chair: Jody Tompson, University of Tampa

MOTIVATIONS AND BARRIERS TO ADULT LEARNERS: THE INFLUENCE OF ECONOMIC "HARD TIMES" ON INTENT TO ENROLL

Sarah B. Kimmel, Mississippi College
Kristena P. Gaylor, Belhaven University
M. Ray Grubbs, Millsaps College

RAISING THE BAR: INCOME TAX EDUCATION AT THE UNDERGRADUATE LEVEL

Janice C. Weber, University of Louisiana Monroe

ON DESIGNING A CASE STUDY COMPETITION FOR A CAPSTONE STRATEGIC MANAGEMENT COURSE

George H. (Jody) Tompson, The University of Tampa

IN YOUR BUSINESS AFTER THE FIRST FIVE YEARS

Timothy Scales, Indiana University East
Marsha Jance, Indiana University East

FOUNDATION OF ROCK OR SAND: THE EFFECT OF AN HONOR CODE, INSTITUTIONAL RELIGIOUS AFFILIATION, AND ETHICS EDUCATION ON THE PERCEIVED ACCEPTABILITY OF CHEATING

Kevin P. Pauli, Mississippi College
Tammy Y. Arthur, Mississippi College
Retha Price, Mississippi College

12:30 PM Thursday March 17th

Carrollton Room

Sponsor: Academy of Business Journal

Real Estate Finance—Global Financial Crisis

Session Chair: Paul McGrath, Purdue University Calumet

VARIABLES EXPLAINING STOCK PRICES IN THE HOUSING SECTOR
Jimmy D. Moss, Lamar University
Gisele Moss, Lamar University

FORECASTING AGGREGATE U.S. MORTGAGE DELINQUENCIES

Paolo Miranda, Purdue University Calumet
Paul McGrath, Purdue University Calumet

MARKET FUNDAMENTALS, SQUARE FOOTAGE, AND BUBBLE BEHAVIOR IN HOUSING PRICES: A FIRST LOOK

Andrew P. Hill, University of Mississippi
Jim Washam, Arkansas State University

FINANCIAL CRISIS AND STOCK MARKET INTEGRATION: REVISITING FAMA-FRENCH MODEL

Ehab Yamani, University of Texas-Arlington

THE LIGHTS ARE OUT AT COMMERCIAL BANKS IN GEORGIA: EXPLAINING BANK FAILURES IN THE 21ST CENTURY

Jill M. Hendrickson, University of St. Thomas
Mark W. Nichols, University of Nevada Reno

Session Chair: T. David Reese, College of Coastal Georgia

INVESTMENT PERFORMANCE AND TRADING PATTERNS OF INDIVIDUAL INVESTORS

Jinwoo Park, Hankuk University of Foreign Studies
Minhyuk Kim, Korea Deposit Insurance Corporation

GOT BETA? A PROFESSIONAL APPLICATION OF INTERPRETING SYSTEMATIC RISK

Reinhold P. Lamb, University of North Florida

ACCESS TO TRADE CREDIT FOR MINORITY-OWNED FIRMS AND DISCRIMINATION: EVIDENCE FROM THE SURVEY OF SMALL BUSINESS FINANCE

T. David Reese, College of Coastal Georgia

ACCESS TO TRADE CREDIT FOR MINORITY-OWNED FIRMS AND DISCRIMINATION: EVIDENCE FROM THE SURVEY OF SMALL BUSINESS FINANCE MARKET REACTION TO EARNINGS ANNOUNCEMENTS

Kyung-Chun Mun, Truman State University

LESSONS FROM WORLDCOM: BERNIE EBBERS' CONTRIBUTIONS TO FINANCIAL REPORTING

Tim Wilson, Texas A&M Commerce
Daniel Edelman, Texas A&M Commerce

12:30 PM Thursday March 17ᵗʰ

Esplanade Room

Sponsor: Trump Entertainment

Management

Session Chair: Isaac Wanasika, University of Northern Colorado

WHEN IS IMITATION THE BEST STRATEGY

Isaac Wanasika, University of Northern Colorado
Suzanne L. Conner, New Mexico State University

SUGGESTIONS TO IMPROVE THE QUALITY OF VIETNAMESE ACCOUNTING SYSTEM

Loi V. Nghiem, University of Labor and Society Affairs
Long Pham, New Mexico State University

IMPACT OF CUSTOMER CHARACTERISTICS ON EMPLOYEES' PROPENSITY TO EXPEDITE COMPLAINT REDRESS – A STUDY IN BANKING SECTOR

Purva G. Hegde Desai, Goa University, India
Nandakumar Mekoth, Goa University, India

AN OPTIMIZATION MODEL TO DEVELOP AN INTEGRATED LOGISTICS NETWORK UNDER PERIODIC DEMAND

Seyed Mohammad Seyed-Hosseini, Iran University of Science and Technology
Lida Tafaghodi Khajavi, Iran University of Science and Technology
Ahmad Makui, Iran University of Science and Technology

2:30 PM Thursday March 17th

Carrollton Room

Sponsor: European Finance Association

Finance

Session Chair: Joseph A. Newman, Auburn University Montgomery

401(k) INVESTING WITH THE THREE ASSET MODEL

Richard Taylor, Arkansas State University
David Kern, Arkansas State University

CONSISTENT WINNERS AND LOSERS

Aziz Wathiainani, York University

DIRECT STOCK PURCHASE PLANS: INVESTOR BOON OR BUST?

Raymond M. Johnson, Auburn University Montgomery
Joseph A. Newman, Auburn University Montgomery

THE SIN-REPUBLICAN DIVIDEND: SIN STOCKS' RETURNS AND POLITICAL CYCLE
Salil K Sarkar, University of Texas at Arlington
Mohammad Riaz Uddin, University of Texas at Arlington

WHY DO FIRMS CONDUCT SEASONAL EQUITY OFFERINGS (SEOS) AND PAY DIVIDENDS SIMULTANEOUSLY? THE ROLE OF DOMINANT SHAREHOLDERS

Duc Anh Ngo, University of Texas El Paso

BANK SECRECY: A COMPROMISE BETWEEN TRANSPARENCY AND INDIVIDUAL RIGHTS
Tim Wilson, Texas A&M Commerce
Daniel Edelman, Texas A&M Commerce

Session Chair: Randall Valentine, Academy of Business Research

PREFERENCE STRUCTURE OF CREDIT RATING AGENCIES

Michael Bowe, University of Manchester, United Kingdom
George Christoudolakis, University of Manchester, United Kingdom
Waseem Larik, University of Manchester, United Kingdom

THE INFLUENCE OF OBEDIENCE PRESSURE ON CFO INTENTIONS TO FRAUDULENTLY MISREPORT

Carol Bishop, Georgia Southwestern State University

THE LINKAGE OF LIQUIDITY, CORPORATE GOVERNANCE, AND FIRM VALUE: EVIDENCE FROM RUSSIA

Wei-Xuan Li, Richard Stockton College of New Jersey
Chia-Sheng Chen, University of New Orleans

THE INFORMATIONAL EFFICIENCY OF THE CORPORATE BOND MARKET: WHAT IS THE ROLE OF TRADING VOLUME?"

Ehab Yamani, University of Texas-Arlington

WHAT DRIVES THE INVESTMENT-BASED STOCK RETURNS: FUNDAMENTALS OR SENTIMENTALS?

Ehab Yamani, University of Texas-Arlington

THE EFFECT OF THE FIRM'S FINANCIAL LEVERAGE ON THE VALUE RELEVANCE OF EARNINGS AND EQUITY BOOK VALUE

Kyung Joo Lee, University Maryland Eastern Shore

2:30 PM Thursday March 17th

Esplanade Room

Sponsor: Social Science Resource Network

Management

Session Chair: John Patrick Orr, Webster University

ECONOMIC CORNERSTONES OF THE CZECH REPUBLIC

J. Kim DeDee, University of Wisconsin Oshkosh

MODERATING FACTORS AFECTING STRATEGY SELECTION TO REACH MINORITY OWNED BUSINESSES

Isaura B. Flores, University of Texas Tyler
Kerrie Ambort, University of Texas Tyler
Marilyn Young, University of Texas Tyler
Gregory Dess, University of Texas Dallas

MANAGEMENT TECHNIQUES AND ITS IMPACT ON RETAIL STORES

Frederick Osadebe, Grambling State University

ORGANIZATIONAL CULTURE PERCEPTIONS AND EMPLOYEE SATISFACTION AFTER A SEPARATION ACQUISITION

Leora Gilboa, Ab Initio
John Patrick Orr, Webster University
Julie Palmer-Schuyler, Webster University
John H. Robinson, Webster University

LEADERSHIP TRAINING IN MNCS: ONE SIZE FITS ALL

Holly B. Tompson, Saint Leo University
George H. (Jody) Tompson, The University of Tampa

26

8:30 AM Friday March 18th

Carrollton Room

Sponsor: AACSB Biz School Jobs

Management

Session Chair: Paul Wilkens, Thomas University

CONSUMER PERCEPTIONS OF THE FAMILY BUSINESS IMAGE

Joy Banner, St. Edwards University

THE EFFECTS OF EARLY CHILDHOOD FAMILY AND LABOR MARKET EXPERIENCE ON ADULT EMPLOYEE ENGAGEMENT AND RETENTION

Wendy Campione, Northern Arizona University

PARTNERING: INITIATING AND SUSTAINING INTRA- AND EXTRA-ORGANIZATION COLLABORATION

T. Roger Manley, Florida Institute of Technology
Wade H. Shaw, Mercer University
Robert C. Manley, Office of the General Counsel, Department of the Navy

STUFF HAPPENS: A MODEL OF THE GROUP LIFE CYCLE

Alan D. Wright, Troy University
Frank Smith, Henderson State University
Anita Williams, Henderson State University

INSTITUTIONAL OWNERSHIP AND CONSERVATISM

Ryan Peterson, Arkansas State University
Jim Whitworth, University of North Carolina-Wilmington

8:30 AM Friday March 18th

Gentilly Room

Sponsor: Trump Hotels International

Marketing

Session Chair: Jenny Swearingen, Thomas University

THE IMPACT OF PERCEPTION FACTORS ON CONSUMER REACTION UNDER PRODUCT RECALLS

Hee-Kwon Jung, Black Hills State University

PERCEPTIONS OF SALESPEOPLE AND A SALES CAREER: A COMPARISON OF U.S., SWISS, AND TURKISH STUDENTS

Charles Quigley, Bryant University
Fahri Karakaya, University of Massachusetts Dartmouth
Frank Bingham, Bryant University
Juerg Hari, Zurich University of Applied Sciences, Switzerland
V. Aslihan Nasir, Bogazici University, Turkey

A SEGMENTATION STUDY OF BEACH RENTAL-BY-OWNER ONLINE INQUIRING CUSTOMERS

William Hill, Mississippi State University Meridian

THE INFLUENCE OF eWOM

Kenneth Henderson, Morehead State University
Barbara Lyons, Morehead State University

A PRELIMINARY STUDY OF HEAVY AND LIGHT USERS OF RETAIL SERVICES

Larry Pleshko, Kuwait University
Sarah Al-Houti, University of Alabama

ARE STUDENTS HARNESSING PROFESSIONAL SOCIAL NETWORKS AS A JOB SEARCH STRATEGY?

Teri L. Root, Southeastern Louisiana University
Kenneth W. Ridgedell, Southeastern Louisiana University
Kimberly D. Mulford, Southeastern Louisiana University

THE X-EFFICIENCY AND PROFITABILITY OF HISPANIC BANKING IN THE UNITED STATES

Russ Kashian, University of Wisconsin Whitewater
Juan Gómez Casillas, University of Wisconsin Whitewater

STRUCTURE-PERFORMANCE RELATION IN NEPALESE BANKING INDUSTRY

Dinesh Gajurel, Kantipur City College Nepal

OPERATING RISK AND ASSET GROWTH: POTENTIAL PREDICTORS OF BANK FAILURE

Raymond M. Johnson, Auburn University Montgomery
Joseph A. Newman, Auburn University Montgomery
Ben McMillan, Auburn University Montgomery

BIDDER GAINS ON ACQUISITION ANNOUNCEMENTS: THE CASE OF INSTANTLY COMPLETED DEALS

Sudip Ghosh, Pennsylvania State University-Berks
Christopher J. Marquette, Central Connecticut State University
Christine Harrington, Central Connecticut State University
Thomas G.E. Williams, Fayetteville State University

THE EFFECTS OF DEFERRED TAXES ON CORPORATE DEBT ISSUES

Christine Harrington, Central Connecticut State University
Donald Trippeer, SUNY Oneonta
Walter Smith, University of Tampa

PUBLIC-GAAP AND PRIVATE-GAAP – SHOULD THERE BE A DIFFERENCE?

John McCallister, University of North Florida

RULE-BASED MORAL REASONING AND CPAs' POLITICAL IDEOLOGY

Kevin Ennis, Mississippi State University Meridian
Paul W. Allen, Mississippi State University Meridian

THE IMPACT OF THE INFORMAL ORGANIZATION IN C.P.A. FIRMS

Pamela H. Church, Rhodes College

SITTING ON A GOLD MINE: THE CURRENT STATE OF THE OIL & GAS INDUSTRY IN SOUTH DAKOTA AND THE POTENTIAL ECONOMIC IMPACT OF THE THREE FORKS-SANISH OIL FORMATION

Dwight E. Denman, Northern State University

A MODEL FOR EXTENDING LEAN/SIX SIGMA FOR BUSINESS PROCESS IMPROVEMENT WITHIN FINANCIAL REPORTING ENVIRONMENTS

Mary McCarthy, Central Connecticut State University
Richard McCarthy, Quinnipiac University

UNDERSTANDING ACCOUNTING INFORMATION

Keith W. Lantz, The University of Texas Pan American

Name	Institution, Country	Day	Page
Adams, Russell	University of Texas at Brownsville, USA	March 16	12
Al-Houti, Sarah	University of Alabama, USA	March 18	30
Allen, Paul W.	Professor Emeritus, Mississippi State University, USA	March 18	32
Alwathainani, Abdulaziz M.	York University, Canada	March 17	24
Ambort, Kerrie	University of Texas at Tyler, USA	March 17	27
Amjad, Hammad	Central Punjab University, Pakistan	March 16	8
Arthur, Tammy Y.	Mississippi College, USA	March 17	20
Banner, Joy	St. Edwards University, USA	March 18	28
Belmasrour, Rochid	Southern University at New Orleans, USA	March 16	9
Bingham, Frank	Bryant University, USA	March 18	30
Bishop, Carol	Georgia Southwestern State University, USA	March 17	25
Boregowda, Satish C.	Miami Dade College, USA	March 16	13
Boulware, Karl D.	University of Alabama, USA	March 16	10
Bowe, Michael	University of Manchester, England	March 17	25
Bulck, Hennie Van	University of South Carolina Sumter, USA	March 16	12
Burke, Kimberly G.	Millsaps College, USA	March 16	13
Byekwaso, Serapio	Verispan University, USA	March 16	10
Campione, Wendy	Northern Arizona University, USA	March 18	28
Casillas, Juan Gómez	University of Wisconsin Whitewater, USA	March 18	31
Chakraborty, Chandana	Montclair State University, USA	March 16	10
Chen, Chia Sheng	University of New Orleans, USA	March 17	25
Christoudolakis, George	University of Manchester, England	March 17	25
Church, Pamela H.	Rhodes College, USA	March 18	32
Conner, Suzanne	New Mexico State University, USA	March 17	23
DeDee, J. Kim	University of Wisconsin Oshkosh, USA	March 17	26
Deloach, James A.	Troy University, USA	March 16	12
Denman, Dwight E.	Northern State University, USA	March 18	32
Dennis, Steven A.	University of North Dakota, USA	March 16	8
Desai, Purva Hegde	Goa University, India	March 17	23
Dess, Gregory	University of Texas at Dallas, USA	March 17	27
Dicle, Mehmet F.	Loyola University New Orleans, USA	March 16	10
Duval-Couetil, Nathalie A.	Miami Dade College, USA	March 16	13
Edelman, Daniel	Texas A&M Commerce, USA	March 17	22
Edelman, Daniel	Texas A&M Commerce, USA	March 17	24
Elahi, Behin	Iran University of Science & Technology, Iran	March 17	17
Elahi, Behin	Iran University of Science & Technology, Iran	March 17	18
Ennis, Kevin L.	Mississippi State University, USA	March 18	32
Fender, Blakely Fox	Millsaps College, USA	March 16	13
Ferguson, Keith	Kennesaw State University, USA	March 17	15
Flores, Isaura B.	University of Texas at Tyler, USA	March 17	27
Fraccastoro, Katherine A.	Lamar University, USA	March 17	15
Funches, Vanessa	Auburn University Montgomery, USA	March 17	15
Gajurel, Dinesh P.	Kantipur City College, Nepal	March 18	31

Ghosh, Sudip	Pennsylvania State University-Berks, USA	March 18	31
Gilboa, Leora	Ab Inito, USA	March 17	27
Gilsinan, James F.	St. Louis University, USA	March 17	18
Grubbs, M. Ray	Millsaps College, USA	March 17	20
Handy, Rodney G.	Miami Dade College, USA	March 16	13
Hari, Juerg	Zurich University of Applied Science, Switzerland	March 18	30
Haile, Semere	Grambling State University, USA	March 17	17
Harrington, Christine	Central Connecticut State University, USA	March 18	31
Harrington, Christine	Central Connecticut State University, USA	March 18	31
Henderson, Kenneth	Morehead State University, USA	March 18	30
Hendrickson, Jill M.	University of St. Thomas, USA	March 17	21
Hill, Andrew P.	University of Mississippi, USA	March 17	21
Hill, William	Mississippi State University Meridian, USA	March 18	30
Hudack, Lawrence R.	Troy University, USA	March 16	12
Ilyas, Bilal	Central Punjab University, Pakistan	March 16	8
Jahanyan, Saeed	Tarbiat Modares University, Iran	March 16	9
Jance, Marsha	Indiana University East, USA	March 17	20
Jensen, Søren H.	Copenhagen Business School, Denmark	March 17	17
Johnson, Raymond M.	Auburn University Montgomery, USA	March 18	31
Johnson, Raymond M.	Auburn University Montgomery, USA	March 17	24
Jung, Hee-Kwon	Black Hills State University, USA	March 18	30
Karakaya, Fahri	University of Massachusetts Dartmouth, USA	March 18	30
Karani, Komal G.	Lamar University, USA	March 17	15
Kashain, Russ	University of Wisconsin Whitewater, USA	March 18	31
Kearney, Terrence J.	Chicago State University, USA	March 17	15
Kern, David F.	Arkansas State University, USA	March 17	24
Khajavi, Lida T.	Iran University of Science & Technology, Iran	March 17	23
Kim, Minhyuk	Korea Deposit Insurance Corporation, South Korea	March 17	22
Kimmel, Sara B.	Mississippi College, USA	March 17	20
Lamb, Reinhold P.	University of North Florida, USA	March 17	22
Lantz, Kieth W.	University of Texas – Pan American, USA	March 18	32
Larik, Waseem	University of Manchester, England	March 17	25
Lee, Kyung Joo	University of Maryland-Eastern Shore, USA	March 17	26
Levendis, John	Loyola University New Orleans, USA	March 16	8
Levendis, John	Loyola University New Orleans, USA	March 16	10
Li, Wei-Xuan	The Richard Stickton College of New Jersy, USA	March 17	25
Lyons, Barbara	Morehead State University, USA	March 18	30
Makui, Ahmad	Iran University of Science & Technology, Iran	March 17	17
Makui, Ahmad	Iran University of Science & Technology, Iran	March 17	18
Makui, Ahmad	Iran University of Science & Technology, Iran	March 17	23
Manley, Robert C.	Department of the Navy, USA	March 18	28
Manley, T. Roger	Florida Institute of Technology, USA	March 18	28
Marquette, Christopher J.	Central Connecticut State University, USA	March 18	31
McAllister, John P.	University of North Florida, USA	March 18	32
McCarthy, Mary	Central Connecticut State University, USA	March 18	32

McGrath, Paul	Purdue University Calumet, USA	March 17	21
McMillan, Ben	Auburn University Montgomery, USA	March 18	31
Mekoth, Nandakumar	Goa University, India	March 17	23
Miah, Muhammed	Southern University New Orleans, USA	March 16	9
Miranda, Paolo	Purdue University Calumet, USA	March 17	21
Moss, Gisele J.	Lamar University, USA	March 17	21
Moss, Jimmy D.	Lamar University, USA	March 17	21
Mulford, Kimberly D.	Southern Louisiana University, USA	March 18	30
Mun, Kyung-Chun	Truman State University, USA	March 17	22
Nasir, V. Aslihan	Bogazici University, Turkey	March 18	30
Nelson, Susan Logan	University of North Dakota, USA	March 16	8
Newman, Joseph A.	Auburn University Montgomery, USA	March 18	31
Newman, Joseph A.	Auburn University Montgomery, USA	March 17	24
Ngheim, Loi V.	University of Labor and Society Affairs, Vietnam	March 17	23
Ngo, Duc Anh	University of Texas at El Paso, USA	March 17	24
Nichols, Mark W.	University of Nevada Reno, USA	March 17	21
Omar, Adnan	Southern University at New Orleans, USA	March 16	9
Onwumere, Remigius U.	St. Louis University, USA	March 17	18
Orr, John Patrick	Webster University, USA	March 17	27
Orr, John Patrick	Webster University, USA	March 18	28
Osadebe, Frederick	Grambling State University, USA	March 17	27
Pae, Sangshin (Sam)	Arkansas State University, USA	March 16	12
Palmer-Schuyler, Julie	Webster University, USA	March 17	27
Palmon, Oded	Rutgers Business School, USA	March 16	10
Park, Jinwoo	Hankuk University of Foreign Studies, South Korea	March 17	22
Parker, Patsy	Southwestern Oklahoma State University, USA	March 16	13
Pauli, Kevin P.	Mississippi College, USA	March 17	20
Pervaiz, Ali	Central Punjab University, Pakistan	March 18	8
Peterson, Ryan	Arkansas State University, USA	March 18	28
Phan, Long	New Mexico State University, USA	March 17	14
Phan, Long	New Mexico State University, USA	March 17	14
Phan, Long	New Mexico State University, USA	March 17	23
Pleshko, Larry P.	Kuwait University, Kuwait	March 18	30
Poulfelt, Flemming	Copenhagen Business School, Denmark	March 17	17
Price, Retha	Mississippi College, USA	March 17	20
Priesmeyer, Richard H.	St. Mary's University, USA	March 17	15
Primont, Diane	Southeast Missouri State University, USA	March 16	8
Quigley, Charles	Bryant University, USA	March 18	30
Quinn, Tina	Arkansas State University, USA	March 16	12
Reed, Robert R.	University of Alabama, USA	March 16	10
Reese, T. David	College of Coastal Georgia, USA	March 17	22
Reich, Robert	Kennesaw State University, USA	March 17	14
Ridgedell, Kenneth W.	Southern Louisiana University, USA	March 18	30
Robinson, John H.	Webster University, USA	March 17	27
Robinson, Richard	Marquette University, USA	March 17	15

Root, Teri L.	Southern Louisiana University, USA	March 18	30
Russell, Doug	Northwest Missouri State University, USA	March 17	16
Safdar, Zubair	Central Punjab University, Pakistan	March 16	8
Saleem, Ayesha	University of Central Punjab, Pakistan	March 17	17
Samizadeh, Reza	Al'Zahra University, Iran	March 16	9
Sarkar, Salil K.	University of Texas at Arlington, USA	March 17	24
Scales, Timothy	Indiana University East, USA	March 17	20
Senarith, Patrick	Miami Dade College, USA	March 16	13
Seyed-Hosseini, Seyed M.	Iran University of Science & Technology, Iran	March 17	17
Seyed-Hosseini, Seyed M.	Iran University of Science & Technology, Iran	March 17	18
Seyed-Hosseini, Seyed M.	Iran University of Science & Technology, Iran	March 17	23
Shaw, Wade H.	Mercer University, USA	March 18	28
Shepp, Larry	Rutgers University, USA	March 16	10
Sheth, Arnav	St. Mary's College of California, USA	March 16	10
Sintim-Aboagye, Hermann	Montclair State University, USA	March 16	10
Smith, Frank	Henderson State University, USA	March 18	28
Smith, Walter	University of Tampa, USA	March 18	31
Soyer, Refik	The George Washington University, USA	March 16	9
Starchan, Beverly J.	Troy University, USA	March 16	12
Summary, Rebecca	Southeast Missouri State University, USA	March 16	8
Taylor, Richard W.	Arkansas State University, USA	March 17	24
Taylor, Susan W.	Millsaps College, USA	March 16	13
Teng, Joe	Troy University, USA	March 16	9
Tompson, George H.	The University of Tampa, USA	March 17	20
Tompson, George H.	The University of Tampa, USA	March 17	27
Tompson, Holly B.	Saint Leo University, USA	March 17	27
Tran, Thang	National Economics University, Vietnam	March 17	14
Tripper, Donald	State University of New York, USA	March 18	31
Uddin, Mohammad R.	University of Texas at Arlington, USA	March 17	24
Uwalaka, Emmanuel	St. Louis University, USA	March 17	18
Valentine, Dawn	Georgia Southwestern State University, USA	March 16	13
Vu, Huong T.	National Economics University, Vietnam	March 17	14
Walker, Jim	Northwest Missouri State University, USA	March 17	15
Wanasika, Isaac	University of Northern Colorado, USA	March 17	23
Warner, Rickey	Grambling State University, USA	March 16	13
Washam, Jim	Arkansas State University, USA	March 17	21
Wathiainani, Aziz	York University, Canada	March 17	24
Weber, Janis	University of Louisiana Monroe, USA	March 17	20
Whitt, Michael D.	Miami Dade College, USA	March 16	13
Whitworth, Jim	University of North Carolina Wilmington, USA	March 18	28
Williams, Anita	Henderson State University, USA	March 18	28
Williams, David	Kennesaw State University, USA	March 17	14
Williams, Donna	Grambling State University, USA	March 17	17
Williams, Thomas G. E.	Fayetteville State University, USA	March 18	31
Wilson, Tim	Texas A&M Commerce, USA	March 17	22

Wilson, Tim	Texas A&M Commerce, USA	March 17	24
Wright, Alan D.	Troy University, USA	March 18	28
Xu, Feng	Georgia Southwestern State University, USA	March 16	9
Yamani, Ehab	University of Texas at Arlington, USA	March 17	21
Yamani, Ehab	University of Texas at Arlington, USA	March 17	25
Yamani, Ehab	University of Texas at Arlington, USA	March 17	25
Young, Marilyn	University of Texas at Tyler, USA	March 17	27

Countries Represented at 2011 Academy of Business Research Spring Conference

Canada
Denmark
India
Iran
Kuwait
Nepal
Netherlands
Pakistan
South Korea
Switzerland
Turkey
United Kingdom
United States
Vietnam

Our next conference will be held September 13-15 2011
Trump Plaza Atlantic City, New Jersey

www.academyofbusinessresearch.com

Academy of Business Research